JABEZ,

PUSHED BY PAIN INTO HIS DESTINY

Lily Chestnut

AuthorHouse™
1663 Liberty Drive
Bloomington, IN 47403
www.authorhouse.com
Phone: 833-262-8899

Because of the dynamic nature of the Internet, any web addresses or links contained in this book may have changed
since publication and may no longer be valid. The views expressed in this work are solely those of the author and do
not necessarily reflect the views of the publisher, and the publisher hereby disclaims any responsibility for them.

Scripture quotations marked NIV are taken from the Holy Bible, New International Version®. NIV®. Copyright ©
1973, 1978, 1984 by International Bible Society. Used by permission of Zondervan. All rights reserved. [Biblica]

Scripture quotations marked NKJV are taken from the New King James Version. Copyright
© 1982 by Thomas Nelson, Inc. Used by permission. All rights reserved.

Scripture quotations marked NLT are taken from the Holy Bible, New Living Translation, copyright © 1996, 2004, 2007.
Used by permission of Tyndale House Publishers, Inc. Carol Stream, Illinois 60188. All rights reserved. Website

This book is printed on acid-free paper.

ISBN: 978-1-6655-5208-0 (sc)
ISBN: 978-1-6655-5207-3 (e)

Library of Congress Control Number: 2022902880

Print information available on the last page.

Published by AuthorHouse 03/28/2022

authorHOUSE®

DEDICATED TO

Anyone who has ever been abused, bullied, or rejected

PRAYER FOR READERS

Heavenly Father,

Thank you for allowing me the privilege to reach out to every reader.

You are such a gracious, loving, all-knowing, and Wise God. You know us better than we know ourselves. Thank you that we can trust you to meet our needs.

Lord, I pray that this book will help uplift anyone who feels lost, lonely, mistreated, rejected or simply needs to be reminded that You, the Almighty God, are still in control regardless of the problems, situations or memories assaulting them. Thank you, Lord, for having the solution even before we get to the problem. Thank you for your mighty power. No one could ever take your place.

Lord, I pray that as each person begins to read, you will let them know that they are loved, wanted, and valued by You, and You are concerned with every facet of their lives.

Open the heart of every reader. Allow them to feel your love flowing through their very being, and Father, not only Your love but let comfort, encouragement, and healing flow through them like a mighty rushing river; so that they will know that You are with them and know you will never leave nor forsake them. Let them feel your presence as You remain their constant companion and guide; please instill that assurance deep within their heart and mind.

For Lord, You are the One who knows and feels every pain and burden that they are carrying. I pray that in the name of Your Son Jesus that You, Almighty God, will surround them with your grace and mercy. Father, fill them with Your peace and joy.

Please help anyone who has experienced hurts, pains, and regrets to release them to You through the vehicle of prayer. Grant every reader the confidence to surrender every issue, holding them captive, and grab onto Your victory for their lives.

Amen

INTRODUCTION

Pain is universal, and no one is exempt from it, regardless of age, wealth, or status. It speaks the same language to all of us without the need for a translator! There are many different types of pain that affect humanity. For example, there are women worldwide who have experienced the pain of childbirth. Childbirth is exclusively a female experience, but life pains affect everyone, regardless of gender, race, nationality, or ethnicity. Everyone has (Or will) deal with the death of a loved one or friend. Millions of other people have dealt with the pain of abuse, divorce, rejection, job loss, foreclosure, etc. The list can go on and on but, whatever the circumstances, there is one thing we all can agree on: Pain is ugly, vicious, and can leave lasting physical, mental, or emotional effects.

Don't underestimate the power of pain. It can turn a 6'5 muscular man into a weeping little boy. Yes, it can indeed wreak havoc in our lives. That is why painkillers are a multibillion-dollar industry because no one wants the pain to be their constant companion. Never mind all the side effects from painkillers; we want relief, and rightly so.

My prayerful desire is for this book to become a spiritual painkiller manufactured by the Word and prayer. All who read it will gain the strength and tenacity they need to allow painful experiences to be a catalyst that will push them into their place of blessings.

JABEZ, PUSHED BY PAIN INTO HIS DESTINY

Now Jabez was more honorable than his brothers, and his mother called his name Jabez, saying, "Because I bore him in pain." 1 Chronicles 4:9

JABEZ, JABEZ, JABEZ

Google "Jabez," and you will find an abundance of literature written about him. Every time there is a new book, the author has discovered something that will uplift and empower the readers to become more confident in every area of their lives.

The first book of Chronicles 4:1-8 discusses Judah's genealogy. Jabez is intertwined in the middle of Judah's genealogy. Strangely enough, there are only two verses that deal with his entire life. Yet, it gives us a good view of how a godly person deals with a situation they had no control over. There is no mention of Jabez's personal information at all.

Another thing that captures our attention is that Jabez's character is described before his identity. I believe this emphasizes who he became more significant than what he was named. Therefore, we get a glimpse into what was and is vital to God. The Almighty is more concerned with who we are than what people label us! People's opinions result from how they perceive you and relate to their own experiences. Fortunately for all of us, God's perception is based on what he sees inwardly.

"For the *Lord does* not *see* as man sees; for man looks at the outward appearance, but the Lord looks at the heart." **1** Samuel 16:7b (NKJV)

According to scripture, Jabez was more honorable than his brothers, yet his mother attached a negative label to his life. Imagine that! It was not his fault that she had experienced such a painful delivery. Still, she blamed Jabez and perceived him in an unfavorable light from birth! Look at how she explains the reason for his name, "and his mother called his name Jabez, saying because I bore him in pain."

What a strange statement for a woman giving birth to her precious baby! You would think she would have looked at her bundle of joy and would have forgotten her labor pains.

In John 16:21(NIV), Christ used the example of childbirth to comfort His disciples concerning His death. "A woman giving birth to a child has pain because her time has come; but when her baby is born, she forgets the anguish because of her joy that a child is born into the world."

Yes, they would experience sorrow but it would not last, just as childbirth pains are replaced with a mother's joy.

BETWEEN LABOR PAINS AND BIRTH

We have very little information about the life of Jabez apart from his character and the reason for his name. However, I cannot help but wonder if, growing up, Jabez possibly had a conversation with his mom; if he did, I believe it would have gone something like this:

"Mom, I was playing with my friends, and some other kids came up and started teasing me." Mom asked, "What were they saying, son?" He responded, they made up a song about me, " Pain, Pain, Jabez, you're nothing but a pain. So, stay away from us, cause you nothing but a pain! After a while mom, even my friends were laughing. Why did you have to name me pain? Even my brothers tease me, especially when I don't do what they want me to. Mom, they make up pain names, and it really hurts! Mom, why? I just don't understand. Nobody else in the family has a name like mine."

"Well, Jabez, when you were born, I was in more pain than I had ever been in with any of your brothers. The pain was so bad that I thought I was going to die! That's why you've got that name. I just couldn't forget the horrible pain and agony."

Jabez's mother was stuck in the memory of her painful experience and made a conscious decision to live in the past. Why do I say it was a conscious decision? Jabez's mother built a negative barrier that blocked all the excitement of having a new baby. She lost sight of her present and had no hope for a happy future with her bouncing baby boy. His mother's painful labor outweighed her joy and caused her to value the pain more than her child. In essence, she filled her mouth with pain language that would forever label her baby on through his adult life. As a result, every time she or anyone else called "Jabez," they were saying, "He will cause pain," which would transport her back into her labor experience. Jabez's mother gave her pain permission to label her as, "Mother of Pain." Every time she looked at her baby, bathed, nursed, washed his clothes, clothed him, or rocked him to sleep, she would relive her experience. It was so sad that a temporary condition caused her to rename her blessing! During biblical times, the birth of a son was considered the highest honor for a woman. A son carried on the posterity of the family name and was the provider of the household. Yet, her past erased that honor from her mind.

As we focused on Jabez's mother, someone important is missing. Yes, you have it right, his father, and we have to wonder why? In those days, the father and sons supported the family. So, why is his father not mentioned? There are so many unanswered questions. For example, did he agree with his wife? Did he try to encourage Jabez? Did the father ever punish Jabez's brothers for making fun of him? I am sure you could probably think of even more questions.

Unfortunately, we will never have the answers to any of these questions. Jabez's dad was an absentee father living with his wife and sons. What is so sad is that even today, the father's voice is silent in many homes. Like Jabez's father, they do not play an active role in their children's lives. Many are great materialistic providers but give little to non-existent emotional support and spiritual guidance. Perhaps had Jabez's father voiced an objection to the name, Jabez would not have experienced the trauma of growing up with a negative label attached to his life.

A DICTATOR CALLED "PAIN"

Let's look at Naomi in the book of Ruth, who had a different type of pain, but the results were the same. Naomi had lost her husband and two sons. She left Moab to return home to her people. Grief blinded Naomi, and she could not see how God was working behind the scene in her life through Ruth, her daughter-in-law. Ruth had refused to return to her people but insisted on following her. When Naomi returned home, people were excited to see her again. So, they said, "Is that Naomi?" (Although she didn't brand a son as Jabez's mother did, Naomi allowed her pain to dictate who she had become and caused her to rename herself.)

Naomi responded, "Don't call me Naomi (pleasant), call me Mara (bitterness). For the Almighty has dealt bitterly with me. I went out full and came back empty" (Ruth 1:20 NKJV)

3

What a pitiful state of mind! It reminds us of the necessity to guard against speaking negative words over ourselves, our family, or situations. When you talk negatively, we allow those words to define who we are or what we expect to happen. I love how the Message Bible interprets Proverbs 18:21.

"Words kill, words give life; they're either poison or fruit—you choose." It's as simple as that. You decide!

Naomi and Jabez's mother decided to choose the adverse road, which led them to view themselves and situations as unfavorable.

REFLECTIONS

THE DANGER OF PAINFUL EXPERIENCES

We can learn from Jabez's mother's life. Her actions scream at us! The danger of embracing painful experiences can cause them to linger in our memories, allowing our pains to distort our view of what God is doing in our lives. Consequently, it results in internal and external damages, taking away our joy and gratefulness. It causes us to remember a temporary condition, which often results in a permanent scar that will continuously nourish any negative thinking.

The real problem is when we allow negativity to take residence in our minds; it becomes difficult to uproot. Whatever enters our hearts will become part of our thought process. Your thought process determines and affects your relationship with God, family, co-workers, and even strangers. Negative thinking will block our blessings, cripple our faith, steal our joy and gratefulness.

SELF-IMPRISONMENT

Philippians 3:13 (NKJV) give us a remedy to holding on to past hurts. "Forgetting those things which are behind and reaching forward to those things which are ahead."

Unfortunately, there is no evidence that Jabez's mother desired to release herself from the prison of past pains and move on with her life.

Instead, she teaches us that if we are unable or unwilling to let go of painful memories, they will consume us, and we will be unable to enjoy any blessings that God birthed out of our pain.

Imagine for a moment getting into your car and driving forward while looking in the rear mirror. I guarantee that you will crash into something or someone in a couple of minutes! Now, apply that same action to the disappointments, betrayals, hurts, struggles, or whatever you have experienced. Let go of those memories, and hurt.

Allow the Holy Spirit to heal your wounds; if there is a need to forgive someone, do it! Forgiveness is not always easy, but it is necessary to fulfill God's plan and purpose for your life. Sometimes it is easy to forget that God sees everything that has ever happened in your life.

In Galatians 6:7, Paul reminds every believer that "God is not mocked; for whatsoever a man sows, that he will also reap." God knows how to handle your haters. Leave them to him. Release yourself from the anger and bitterness through the power of prayer and faith in God's ability to manage your business.

If you need someone to forgive you, ask them. It does not matter if the person or persons reject your apology; God knows when you are genuinely sorry, and He accepts the apology on their behalf. What a merciful and gracious God!

Perhaps your hurt stems from suppressed anger over how someone who is deceased treated you. Do yourself a favor, go to God and ask him to release you from that infested resentment. Then sincerely forgive that person. Realize that the enemy wants you to hold onto your painful past so that those memories can imprison you and hinder your spiritual and emotional well-being. Remember, that storm has ended! So, pull your emotions out, refuse to live in those memories, and move with your life!

JABEZ'S CHARACTER

Jabez's character was more honorable than his brothers. The Bible does not deal with his childhood or adolescent years but jumps directly to his adult life. The verse describes Jabez as more honorable than his brothers. In other words, he had become a better person than all of his siblings—a person of integrity, a godly man, and dependable. Yet, he was well aware of the curse associated with his name.

What is so unique about Jabez is that he refused to allow his mother's experience to dictate and define who he was or would become. He must have thought; my mama prediction will never come to pass in my life. It did not matter that it was his mom, the closest person to him; he still would not accept it as the final word in his life.

STOP RIGHT HERE- FOOD FOR THOUGHT

Jabez, through his actions, demonstrates a truth to every person who is facing negativity from people who are closest to them and should have their best interest at heart; unfortunately, sometimes that is the individual or individuals Satan is using against them.

Psalm 55:12-13(NLT) bears out this truth
   "It is not an enemy who taunts me—
   I could bear that. It is not my foes who so arrogantly insult me—
   I could have hidden from them.13 Instead, it is you—my equal,
   my companion, and close friend."

LET'S GET BACK TO JABEZ

What does Jabez decide to do to negate and destroy this prophecy over his life? He turns to God and uses the pain and negativity surrounding him to push himself into his destiny.

It is easy to surmise that Jabez had more than a causal relationship with God. You can sense the warm confidence he must have felt as he prayed for help. Jabez realized that only God had the power to erase the label and prevent it from becoming the reality of his life.

Jabez teaches us a valuable lesson. We cannot allow anyone to define or predict who you will become according to their experiences. However, by having a personal relationship with God, you can boldly go to Him for His guidance. Why it is so imperative to make certain our connection is authentic.

Imagine having a friend, but you are always busy and can only engage in a two or three-minute conversation twice a month. The person even attempts to catch up with you other times, but you are never available. What both of you have is not a real friendship, just a casual relationship.

God does not want to be your casual acquaintance. He desires to have a personal relationship with every one of his children. A relationship that creates a faith-built connection so His power can flow to and through our lives.

John 15:7 NKJV states, "If you abide in Me, and My words abide in you, you will ask what you desire, and it shall be done for you."

Yes, a genuine relationship with the Father has a Guaranteed Answer and Lifetime Warranty.

And Jabez called on the God of Israel saying, "Oh, that You would bless me indeed, and enlarge my [a]territory, that Your hand would be with me, and that You would keep *me* from evil, that I may not cause pain!" So God granted him what he requested. 1 Chronicles 4:10 (NKJV)

Jabez's prayer has four requests:

An Indeed Blessing

"Oh, that you would bless me indeed."

According to dictionary.com, the word bless means favor or gift bestowed by God, thereby bringing happiness. Jabez asked God to lift him demonstrate His favor on his life. He needed a blessing that would change his life forever. This blessing would stand in sharp contrast to his mother's actions in his life.

I believe his faith grabs God's attention. Jabez had made God the top priority in his life. His fellowship with the Almighty helped Jabez develop the trust and confidence to trust God as his source of blessings. The only ONE who could stamp out the evil spoken against him and exalt him above his family and friends.

Yes, Jabez teaches us to believe and trust that God hears and will answer. We are in partnership with God. He only does what we are unable to do. Imagine a person praying for a job but never sends out a resume nor speaks to anyone

who might know about open positions. They may pray, even become discouraged, and complain to God, but no avail! James reminds us that "faith without works is dead" James 2:26b (NKJV)

Jabez's faith caused him to pray, that was his works, and it must be ours as well.

Once we have prayed and put our impossibilities into the hands of the One who knows no impossibilities, victory is assured!

2. A BLESSING OF ENLARGEMENT

"And enlarge my territory."

Don't you just love Jabez? I do. Jabez was not satisfied with his present situation. He wanted an increase, more growth in his life, and I believe Jabez saw an increase in his Spirit even before he requested it.

If Jabez could speak today, he would tell you: See yourself coming out, see yourself healed, see yourself debt-free and see yourself victorious!

We don't know why Jabez requested a boundary increase. Perhaps he had received a lesser portion of land than his brothers. But whatever the situation was, Jabez's possessions did not reflect his true self. Although his name had probably disadvantaged him in his family and community, he was not discouraged, angry, or depressed.

Jabez speaks volumes to us; possessions do not always reflect who God has made us or who we will become. We must believe in ourselves and God's power because we are victors and not victims!

The scripture acknowledged him as more honorable than his brothers, which leads me to believe that Jabez did not fit into their lifestyle. He was a misfit with a negative label, but it did not change his perception of himself or his confidence in God's love and acceptance of him

Unfortunately, there will be times when you will not fit into the lifestyle practices of those closest to you. As a result, you may often find yourself being shunned, criticized, or overlooked, and it will hurt, but be encouraged and don't be afraid to be a misfit. It just means that God has chosen you for greatness in Him!

Joseph was a misfit among his brothers, and they hated him and his dreams, but God allowed him to become governor of Egypt. The only person higher than him was the Pharoah! (Genesis 41:37-39)

The excellent news is Jabez demonstrated what a true child of God must do. He remained steadfast, honorable, and encouraged amid discouragement, negativity, and pain.

Jabez's request was not selfish, and God knew that because He understood Jabez's intentions. God also knew Jabez would never allow a blessing to destroy his godly character; and that his servant would always give Him the glory and credit for every gift. God trusted Jabez.

"Isn't it good when God can trust you with a blessing?"

When I was a young adult, a young woman (I will call Mary) joined our small church and gave her life to the Lord. She joined the choir and the youth group. She was friendly and well-liked, and one of the best singers in our choir. After a year or so, God miraculously allowed her to meet someone who introduced her to an opportunity that allowed Mary to receive free training for a well-paying position. She could have never obtained that position on her own merits or educational background. Everyone was excited for her because it was indeed a miracle. Mary faithfully attended services, Bible studies, and choir rehearsals for about a couple of years.

Eventually, she began to receive incredible salary increases, and something changed! She stopped regularly attending services, stopped singing with the choir, and socializing with the other young people. Finally, she dropped out of the church, choir, youth group and reverted to her old habits.

The problem was that she thought she was ready for that blessing, but she was not. Through God's mercy, He had given her an incredible testimony, but unlike Jabez, God could not trust her to stay faithful to Him. After some time, she lost the job and eventually returned to the Lord, but she never received such an incredible opportunity again.

In His heart, Jabez knew that he was ready to receive more from the God he served. I also believed he had a legitimate requirement for a larger territory. Perhaps he had unjustly received a smaller portion than his brothers. Whatever the reason, Jabez knew God could change his situation.

For believers, our territories are the various needs in our lives. Our necessities vary according to our areas of lack. It can be healing, finances, job opportunities, family or marital problems, etc. Whatever the situation, it does not matter because God already knows about it and has the solution.

That is why the scripture encourages, "So let us come boldly to the throne of our gracious God. There we will receive his mercy, and we will find grace to help us when we need it most." (Hebrews 4:12 (NLT)

3. THE BLESSING OF GOD'S PRESENCE

"That your hand will be with me."

Jabez said God, I do not want your blessing without your presence and power. He understood that in God's presence, there would be peace, protection, and God-ordained prosperity.

We must be like Jabez in our desire for God's presence in our lives for the same three reasons: His Presence, Protection, and God-ordained prosperity.

His presence is necessary for every child of God because true contentment and joy are impossible without His presence.

Psalm 16:11 says, "You make known to me the path of life, in your presence, there is fullness of joy; at your right hand are pleasures forevermore."

Secondly, we can depend on Him to protect us from the enemy's attacks. Never forget that Satan wants to destroy us because he hates God. What better way to get back at the Almighty? Christ made it clear to us that Satan came to steal, kill and destroy" (John 10:10 NKJV)

Thirdly, God-Ordained Prosperity, I believe, is more important than having millions in the bank; because financial well-being-without God is empty and cannot satisfy the soul. Some of the most miserable people have enormous wealth.

4. THE BLESSING OF GOD'S PROTECTION

"And that you will keep me from the evil that I may not cause pain."

What an extraordinary request! Jabez tapped into the stigma that hung over his life. Jabez's name was a painful reminder of the negativity in his life, which labeled him a person who would always cause hurt wherever he went. Now, Jabez had the confidence and faith to petition His God. His greatest desire was to have the cursed label nullified and removed from his life. He understood that he was not responsible for his mother's feelings and refused to accept the negativity any longer. Jabez shows us his heart through his request. He has no desire to do anything that would cause anyone to suffer. Jabez makes it clear that he does not want to live any longer overshadowed by the dictates of his mother's mouth. He understood that he did not have any power over what his mother named him, but he could seek God for his destiny. He was determined to live a blessed life and be a blessing to those around him.

GOD GRANTED HIM HIS REQUEST.

Jabez's story encourages anyone who feels their childhood experiences or society has unjustly labeled them.

Jabez refused to become a reflection of his name. Nor would he allow himself to harbor bitterness in his heart. He could have easily hated his mother and become a bitter, hateful person. But, no, instead of anger and hatred, Jabez ripped his mother's label off through prayer, and you can do the same thing. Sincere prayer will give you the strength to rip the labels, people and situations, family backgrounds, etc., have placed on you. Labels that proclaim: not good enough, failure, worthless, dumb, unloved, unwanted, a mistake, or any other label the enemy tries to attach to your life. Remember, Jabez demonstrates that your pain will fuel your prayer and that prayer can change anything in your life and push you into your destiny of abundant living.

Jabez reminds us to use our painful experiences as a catalyst to grab God's attention because He is always available. So, whatever you encounter in this life journey, remember to let your pain push you into your victorious destiny!

REFLECTIONS

HEAVENLY FATHER,

I praise You for who You are. You are the God who knows everything; you are well acquainted with my ways. You alone know my uprisings, down sitting, and even my thoughts afar off. Nothing I say, do, or think is hidden from You. Lord, that's why I turn to You for strength. Mold me and shape me according to Your will and purpose for my life.

Lord God, I don't want to be left to my own devices.

Guide my path, lead me in the direction of peace, joy, and prosperity—You and You alone control my destiny. I am glad to know no one could ever take Your place.

Please grant me the tenacity to stand amid adversities. Thank you for loving me beyond my pain. Help me not allow bitterness, hatred, and unforgiveness to my spirit. Lord, empower me to walk in love and with a forgiving heart and let my life be evident to all of your grace and mercy.

And Lord _____

_____

_____

_____

_____

_____

_____

_____

Printed in the United States
by Baker & Taylor Publisher Services